Ten Love Poems & an Unknown Number

by

Rudy Thomas

OLD SEVENTY CREEK PRESS

COPYRIGHT 2014 BY Rudy Thomas

**2014 OLD SEVENTY CREEK PRESS
FIRST EDITION**

PUBLISHED IN THE UNITED STATES
BY OLD SEVENTY CREEK PRESS
RUDY THOMAS, PUBLISHER
P. O. BOX 204
ALBANY, KENTUCKY 42602

**ISBN-13:
978-0615948140 (Old Seventy Creek Press)**

**ISBN-10:
0615948146**

Contents

Stranger in their house

I can imagine the things
they say about me.
I have come to their house
for the second time.
I was here in April.
I am here now in August.
I will be here until September 1st.

When I was in 11 Miles Bull Bay
in April, I was healthy, active.
I spent 4 days & 5 nights in Ocho Rios.
I drank Campari & mango juice.
By the second day, I had other tourists
drinking the same drink.
They began to recognize me as the man
who introduced them to a new mixed drink
& most of them would smile at me
or salute me with a frosted glass.

I am back in 11 Miles Bull Bay
to obtain a student visa
for a 16 year old.
I have told my children
that I have empty nest syndrome,
but the truth is:
I want to give her hope
& a chance for a future.
The family does not know
what they will do with her
when she graduates Vauxhall High.

As for what I imagine that they say, they call
me a rich American. I can understand such

reasoning, for I own 5 cars & pay 3
mortgages. I have running water in my house
& commodes that flush & two showers.

I count 21 family members
in the house on most occasions.
The young student has been with
her aunty for 8 years. She has been raised
as a Christian & her manners are impeccable.
I buy food & cook strange dishes
which they do not enjoy
as much as they do chicken,
rice & peas or oxtail soup
or rice & chicken foot soup.

I imagine that they think
I am lazy. I sleep often.
I do not tell anyone until my last night
that I had 21 needle biopsies
done on my prostate 2 days before I flew
from Nashville to Norman Manley
International airport. I do not tell them that I
bleed like a woman on the worst days of her
period. I do not confess that I am sorrowed
by all that women endure during those days.

I am a stranger in their house,
but I am also a God send.
They pray for me
& thank God for bringing me
to them & offering their granddaughter,
niece, cousin,
all the opportunities that they hear about
from other family & friends
who have gone to foreign.

September 2013, Jamaica

To see the sad faces at the bus stop,
onlookers might think there was
underway a withdrawal from 11 Miles
Bull Bay of all its children,
following the music of a foreign piper.

A land where gangs & the unemployed
outnumber jobs & workers, but a land
held together by maternal threads,
so is Jamaica on the day we go
to Norman Manley International airport.

A land where the wheels of politics
creates a population longing to go
to America, heralded as the land
of opportunity in spite of its sad
economic state, so is Jamaica.

Your sadness has nothing
to do with politics, economies,
or of parties in downtown Kingston.
Bull Bay is still home & family
& friends & a lover, you cherish.

Impromptu Scribbling

You sit on the arm of the sofa.
I sit on the love seat to your left.
You kick off your sandals
& place your right foot
on my left leg—your left toes
on my right leg.

I find a poem in such actions.
My poetry begins when life moves,
rapidly becoming a river of emotions.
Your skin is soft beneath my fingers.
I search it for words. Images & rhyme
surface upon the deep pool of the page.

Downtown Hottie

This poem is for the
6 year old mare
that dumped
her jockey
out of the gate
& outran
all the males
to cross the finish line
first by a length & a half.

May it be
the wreath of roses
placed
around her neck
to take the place
of the one
she never got
at Belmont
on a fast track.

Painting

On this Sunday morning, I stay home.
I study the white canvas on the easel as
tho it were a white sheet of paper
in need of words, a poem to say the least.

Yesterday was the movable feast
my brother-in-law holds annually. The caper
gets family together whereas
other gatherings cannot. Water & sea foam

come to mind as I stare into my soul.
I will paint water falling down on two
naked people, male & female. You & I
near Ocho Rios before we wed.

We laughed, touched, splashed & you said
words of love you did not mean, but words I
took to heart. Moments betrayed by you
I cannot forgive. As for me, I am less whole.

Sevens

At seven past midnight I
sit up on my bed & watch
lightning flash in the southeast.

I count to seven before
I hear thunder. Seven miles
away I tell myself all

the while wanting to hold you.

The Arrival of spring

It is all in feelings
I will say to you
& has nothing to do with logic.

The arrivals of spring, & winter aconite
blooming thru snow, have
nothing to do with logic.

I want to take you in my arms & say
love is insanity, but I dare not say it,
for love has everything to do with feelings

& very little to do with logic.

Watching the Rain

Watching the Rain,
I think of you,

my dead brother.
You once asked

our sister
why I never wrote

about you.
I did not know

you read
my work.

I wrote about you
after that.

I don't think
you ever knew that.

It was a poem about a good day
to be on Lake Cumberland

in a boat
or on the bank

for hours,
watching the water level rise

or feeling the boat rock
as we drift with the flow.

Olive Garden

I beg my leave of the two of you
& make my way to the restroom.

I go to the urinal,
pressure building for a release.

I close my eyes
& breathe deeply.

When I open my eyes,
I see a blond haired girl's head

tilted inward
& slightly upward.

I look over my right shoulder
& see the embarrassed father

rushing toward the young girl.
He pulls her backward, saying nothing.

"He's got one of those, too, Daddy,"
the young girl says.

The father shoos her toward the door
like a farmer trying to get a pig

or a calf to find the hole in a fence
where it got out.

She dashes under his arms
but does not elude them.

September Day

Seven geese fly south.
Cool weather will follow.
It is as it has always been.

I am as I have been as well.
I will confess in words
nothing more than that.

Naked Ladies

As (swiftly) summer ends,
you sleep this September
Sunday morning.

Two tomatoes (washed),
stickers removed,
await your eyes.

I will slice one (the ripest)
& toast two slices
of wheat bread.

Such will be your brunch.
My words (written)
will be a poem.

While (deeply) I slept,
ladies intrigued me
in a dream explicit.

In it, one (not the lot)
wore fine clothes.
I unloved her again.

The others (amaryllis)
I reached for with open arms
only to embrace emptiness.

Love Poem 1

After three months
of seeing you

& hearing your voice,
I embrace you

with words
& feelings flow

thru me
like Old Seventy Creek

in a time of drought.
We sway

like dancers
& I wonder

whether you realize
I am writing this poem at all.

Love Poem 2

Last evening
before dusk
before rain
falls,

Mockingbird
sits on the wire
above my driveway
& sings.

The neighbor's
black cat
crosses the road
en route to my yard.

The Mockingbird
swoops down
& buries her bill
in the cat's neck.

The cat tucks
its tail & runs home,
the Mockingbird
in hot pursuit.

I know the eggs
have hatched
in the Hawthorne
by the lilies.

I walk to the tree
& see three
featherless heads
upright with beaks open.

The Mockingbird
scolds me from the wire
but does not attack.
She does not fear me.

She follows me
when I mow
& catches
insects.

As they ripen,
I let her harvest
mulberries, cherries,
& blue berries.

It must appear
to her that
I raise such delicacies
only out of love.

Love Poem 3

Look at us.
we have taken

the first steps
toward poetry.

We know
what secrets

lurk in the dark
& which words

can be exposed
to a white page.

Love Poem 4

On this
not a typical morning
I sit on the edge of the bed
while it is yet dark
& I long to touch you.

After daylight
on this
not a typical morning
I work out at the gym
with a group of students.

I skip breakfast
on this
not a typical morning
& create a butterfly on a painting
I thought I had finished.

On this
not a typical morning
I remember my brother
& how in his dying
he told me he loved me

for the
first
last
& only time
in our lives.

Love Poem 5

Getting back to you last night,
& a love poem, you take off
to talk on your phone during the movie
which is not unusual. For a short time,
however, you slip the fingers
of your left hand
beneath the strap
over your right shoulder.

You pull the strap
of your tank top
away from me,
unaware that you
trigger strong feelings.
I admire your amber skin
& the contour of your breast.

You remove your fingers slowly,
slowly.
I take them in my left hand.
You offer no resistance.
I lean toward you,
pull your hand toward my lips
& kiss the bend of your wrist.

Why do you kiss like that? **you ask.**

Love Poem 6

Your family in Jamaica has no interest in the
words that flood my verses while they sleep.
My voice never pierces through their ears.
As for my rhymes, overloaded trucks drown
out such whispered musings.

May we abide within our separate feelings
while they dream on tethered down
& take their different courses free of fears.
May the full silence of our rooms keep
us steadfast in our resolve & may my poetry

be not of you with them but you with me.

Love Poem 7

After I rise,
it's a hot, blue sky day
of summer & I'm inside the mall
cooling off when I decide to go
to Victoria's Secret,
not meaning to buy 6 panties for one price,
not meaning to rummage through 800+
styles of swim wear, priced up to 50% off.
I don't care at all that the Semi-Annual
Clearance sale ends Tuesday or that for
a limited time I can order you something
& if my purchase is a total of $50,
I can have the item(s) mailed to you
for free.
I enter the store
& straightway a dark-hair
young clerk approaches.

"May I help you with something, sir?"
she asks.
I won't go into details on how good
she looked, suffice it to say
beautiful, a word Robert Frost refused
to use in his poetry.

I always ask for the same item
when I go to Victoria's Secret.
Today was no exception.

"I want Victoria without any secrets,"
I say.

I did not expect her to react as she did.

"I can't help you get Victoria
without her secrets, sir,
but I do know Victoria's secret,"
she said.

"& what might that be?" I ask.

She leans close and whispers in my ear.

& that's why I bought you what I did
for your birthday.

I have yet to ask you
what you think of that gift,
for I have not seen you in months.

Love Poem 8

I read an editor's
submission guidelines:

We almost never
publish verse that is
overtly sexual, self-therapeutic,
or too self-consciously
about poets writing poetry.

We have a deep suspicion
of the personal pronoun,
and of poets who want
to tell us how they feel
about anything in particular.

The guidelines do not cause me
to want to burn my words.
I have always been one to write
of such forbidden things
when I touch a woman.

Love Poem 9

As we leave *Fiesta Mexico,*
I open the door for you
& you say:

I was hungry.
They took too long
to bring our food.

Love Poem 10

So
you are willing
to allow me to put words
before you
in a series of lines,
stanzas,
& images,
that succor my
struggle of turning
outward everything
internal so they become a rushing
like Old Seventy Creek after
rain?

If so,
you must be willing
to understand that my words
will wrap around all of you
both the sensuous (many lines)
& the rational (no stanzas)
& give form to my
aesthetic yearning
to touch you
& know this:
you risk unbridled gushing
poetic after
such pain.

How long forever takes

The moment I see the floating leaf
as a found poem from Ocho Rios
the time you lie
naked on a queen size bed
& I rest my chin
on the mattress,
my knees on the floor.

It is more
or less
six months later when
I realize the watershed
called Old Seventy Creek is my
page. On it, I write words for you, Ocho Rios,
the floating leaf & how I shake your belief--

your concept of how long forever takes.

Colors—A Fractured Rhyme Scheme

Like the Character, David,
in the movie, *Vanilla Sky,*
I have lucid dreams about you
throughout the night.

I dream in colors, vivid
amber brown like the eye
you wink at me as you
sit to my right,

your body warmed by
an electric blanket.
I dream of you in the country,
surrounded by green Jamaican

flora and fauna, Jamaican
blue sea, & a red fruited ackee,
above an uncultivated heath,
touching a clear & endless sky.

I dream of the game, *Purple Touch,*
& the way you explained it. You say,
"When a man catches a woman
away from a tree, he can touch her

anywhere he pleases." Your words stir
the poet in me. I chase you, woman.
Your beauty is clothed in black Bull Bay
night. I catch you. I say, "Purple Touch."

I touch you where I must to get
the word best suited for my poem.
It swells, is warm & nervous wet.

Porcelain & glaze

You are nude.
I paint you
the way God made woman,
then placed her with man in a Garden.

I do not paint you lewd
on white canvas. You,
like Old Seventy Creek in sun-
light, are overshadowed by no garden.

You will recognize you are
the model I portray.
The landscape is unimportant.
The birds are not audible.

The horizon disappears far
from your eyes, their sway,
their dance, their full front
& center look, a sensible,

sensuous gaze.

Beneath a stone

I like it best when a word emerges
in unexpected moments,
as did the bear wallows in Franklin fields,
& the woods grouse rising suddenly
in twilight, disappearing on whistling wings.

I like best the word that sings
of Old Seventy Creek, lazily
flowing & involuntarily yields
a thought, a longing for you, a crescent
moon in its first quarter. My intimate urges

hide like a snail darter beneath a stone.

A Game of Scents

You put your finger under my nose.
It smells worse than yesterday's garbage.

I wonder where you have put it
to capture such decadence.

You laugh & threaten my nose again.

I rub my finger down your cleavage
to pick up the scent of a red, red rose

that Robert Burns loved as poet
& having done it once,

I threaten to do it, & do it again.

Night

I lie awake.
I hear you call out.

I don't distinguish the words,
but I am not dreaming.

I rise quickly.
I sit on your bed.

You sleep like a child
in a fetal position.

I want to touch you.
I do not.

I dare not wake you.
I gather my feelings

about me like you have
tucked your electric blanket

across & around
you slender body.

I sit on your bed,
silent in the soft glow

of your night light
while my shadow clings to you.

A skiff of snow

A skiff of snow fell
silently from early morning,
all the while
a light wind blowing.

Tho I long to tell
you it has snowed, no warning
do I risk. You will smile
when you discover it is snowing.

At work, I will sit alone,
aching to touch you
as I write a poem of warm fingers
moving against warmer skin

& when
a certain feeling lingers
like morning dew
upon fescue and stone,

the skiff of snow
will be gone.

Winter Morning

On a cold November day
in Kentucky,
I scrape rice from your plate
onto a mounting pile of grain
from previous meals.

In 11 Miles Bull Bay,
Jamica, pigeons lucky
enough to land first, relate
a coo with each peck of grain,
& Grassquits perch on window sills.

It seems odd to me
that neither stray dog nor cat,
nor opossum on nightly visits,
nor sparrow, nor Blue Jay,
nor God forbid—a rat, partakes of rice.

Moth

We ride upon
its fragile wings.

It flies toward
open flames

& circles one
growing bolder.

We can only hope
that it remembers us,

for we are lovers
aboard: yet,

true to its nature,
it flies

straightway
toward the light

in search
of itself.

Soft places

When I ask you
if you have soft places
for me,

you hesitate,
want to know
what I mean?

When I tell you,
you understand
how bad memories

are uncomfortable
& all the while,
I consider

how Old Seventy creek,
begins in mystery,
& how fog rises from it,

how the holes pool
in the shade where the stream
joins from the McFarlane farm,

how the cave toward the end
of its course supplies more
clear, cold water,

how wild flowers
grow on the cliffs,
how song birds love it.

The stream writes poetry
onto my memory;
its voice singing from the ripples,

moving like fingers
that create gooseflesh
when they touch warm skin.

Were you the one?

Were you the one in my dream?
If so, what did I say?
I know I snore, & talk at night
while I sleep.

Was Old Seventy Creek the stream
we swam in, naked as newborns? A day
in the water, in the dream, as twilight
fell like words seeking a poem. Did I peep

at your body or stare like a fool
who had never seen a woman nude before?
I did not see your face whatsoever,
if, indeed, you were there beside me.

Always lovely, deep & cold, the pool
is etched in my memory. The more
I try to paint the face, however,
the less sure I am that is you with me.

When I wake, we are two
people on a sofa before dawn.
I hold your feet. You
wear your face. I am drawn

to it like a potted plant to sunlight.

A Poem

I know the length of Old Seventy Creek
from its source to the point
where it sinks
to rise again
& I know where it dies
leaping into Lake Cumberland.

I know the weight of words
the fevered breath of a woman
the length of her legs
the pink tipped roundness she hides
the smell of a poem on her thighs
& the light in her unblinking eyes.

Her poem floats off,
a leaf in the flow of water,
& people will say of it
it is too difficult to read
& understand.

I say forget about understanding.
Touch it!
If it feels like a woman,
a tear on a cheek,
Old Seventy Creek,
or rain,
or a leaf
then that is the sum of it.

When your eyes blink

the thought I have
keeps on
flowing like Old Seventy Creek
across the landscape
of my mind

downward
gathering speed
pooling for a moment
as it tries to turn
back on itself
but it cannot return
nor can I.

When your eyes open
again, you see me,
as Old Seventy Creek,
at the edge
of the limestone cliff

as I become the misty
water-
f
a
l
l
s

I feel the chill

of winter along Old Seventy Creek
on Sunday morning where
the sun disappears & song birds cry
out for warm rays to filter between bare faces
of hardwood trees.
The chill rides a winter cold breeze
reminiscent of tourists leaving
Grider Hill dock
after Labor Day.

I know this winter chill
climbs Grider Mountain, meek,
rounded, & older than the Rockies. There
is no way for me to ignore the how & why
of nature or its secret places
near Lake Cumberland? Who sees
me seize
a life full of poetry less thieving
than winter if not I, a product of hardy stock
like June apples? I play

where rare birds forage
to find their songs—where snail darters
perfect their rhythms & then I confront
the white page
& cast out my words.

Do not frown,

girl,
if I pick you up
twirl you about
& put you
inside a poem
more than one time.

You are the rhyme
in every poem
the rhythm too
& my heart cries out,
my feelings dance with each up

twirl
& put down.

Gypsy

The Southern seas
off Italy
remind me of Greece,
sun glimmering
across your face,
warming the beaches.

The boat drifts
in a time of dreaming
& I am half asleep
& the dances
in your land
of south

are wild
gypsy like
& the organ grinder
sends his monkey
around to beg
for coins.

Such is your street
& a hawk
with short wings
& long legs
darts
in & out

among my trees
in the silent
red of dawning.

In the Darkness

I would hunt in late October
among tall trees above Upchurch Hollow
& listen to my black-and-tan hound
beneath Sewell Bluff when he struck the
scent of a raccoon, fat on acorns.

That hound was a poet.
His voice would echo down the ridges
& cross the distant highway to the north
& then go out of hearing on Williams Creek.
His locating bark would lift me up.

I would climb upward,
leaves crackling under my feet.
Sometimes the old hound would
stop barking & I would stop walking
until he'd catch his breath.

As improbable as it might seem
to anyone who never coon hunted
in late October, climbing upward
in a bent forward run, I still hear
that old dog's poetry in the darkness

of my room.

On warm days

I would sit
under the rock

shelter
where Old Seventy

Creek emerged.

If I sat long
enough

to leave thoughts
of swimming

underwater,

I would go
back in time

& Indians would
emerge from the cave,

but no male nor female

would climb the steep hillside
& joined me.

I was always as invisible
as the bats asleep upside down

in their underground cavern.

December on Campus

It is cold inside my office today.
To balance the school's administrative
budget, all offices have had new thermostats
installed, preset to 70 degrees.

I shiver, my fingers chilled, the freeze
outside comes inside like gnats
through a screen, like water thru a sieve.
I daydream of you. You are in the spillway

of a creek, It does not freeze in winter. Warm,
white water splashes over you & around
the curves of your body. Your white tee
clings to your breasts, & reveals everything

beneath it & your smile is a love song I sing
silently, my feelings saturated. If I could be
there, sitting on a boulder in the background,
I'd fill a gesso canvas with your playful form,

erotic & so mysterious.

Tell me

as I sit on the edge of your bed
that you will love me
if I write my dreams
on your warm skin no matter that
my dreams are unbridled
wild horses racing thru the dark
toward the eastern sky of dawn
where close to a slender waning
crescent moon, Mercury hides.

This morning as you wake tell me
where you will write your dreams,
but not what they are about, for they are
nothing but the fairy tale you want with him
that you keep believing.
You have no desire to view
the evening skies ablaze with planets: Venus,
Mars, & Saturn, shining brightly.
Jupiter is also visible, but dropping rapidly
behind the sun.

But if I am wrong & you want to see Mercury,
& if your dreams are unbridled
wild horses unable to stop
on the edge of dawn & dark,
do not fear for them. Ride one that knows
how to go on or turn back,
but if you are too inexperienced to ride
toward love & outdistance the sex
you had with him while your cousin watched
thru the glass then do not ride at all.

Haystacks in Bright Sunlight

When I was seven,
my grandfather & I
rode in his wagon
pulled by Bill & Diner.

We got to the flat field
in late morning
& began to load oats
in bright sunlight

We loaded the wagon
with pitchforks
(mine with wooden prongs)
& began our first stack.

Our stack grew up a pole.
It was not shaped
like a tribal hut
in a Kenyan village.

I had seen those huts
in my geography book.
The flat field landscape
became a painting.

Impressionistic colors reached
beyond the trees,
past Lake Cumberland
into a clouding sky.

When I was eight,
my grandfather had moved
from the hollow

to Cartwright Mountain.

His large family
could drive up
to his front porch
& visit him after his stroke.

We watched Sputnik
go into space
on his television,
but he did not get out of bed.

My father bought his farm
at the courthouse door
after he died.
A neighbor bid against him.

We took down the hay poles
& fed hay into a baler
with a gas engine
& the mule, Diner, had died.

Dust filled the air
as the baler rammed in oats
& sweat rolled down our faces
in the bright sunlight.

Sunday

When I was 12,
maybe 13,
I went to Mt. Union,
the church on the hill
above Old Seventy Creek.

The minister's
mother-in-law
told me I should go
to the young peoples'
class taught
by the minister's
wife.

I went to her class.
I liked it.
She did not give us
pictures to color.
She did not ask me
to recite Bible verses.

My father took us,
a family of 6,
to visit the minister
on Sunday afternoon.
Father called the minister
Wild Bill.
It was some time later
that I learned why.

When the minister opened
the kitchen door,
I saw his wife,

ironing a white shirt.
I would not have thought
anything negative about that
if she had not said,
"Don't tell anyone
you saw me ironing
on Sunday."

Father must have seen
how lost I was
for an answer.

He said, "He won't whisper
a word of it
if you don't tell anyone
he milked cows,
slopped the hogs,
fed the chickens
& the dogs
this morning."

"Your secret's safe
with me," she said
& it has taken me
these long years
to betray hers
if betrayal is what it is.

You lie on the couch, waiting

I touch you, loving you with my fingers.
I touch you & the memory of loving the
wrong woman burns me as I pull the electric
blanket upward to cover your shoulder.
You sigh, & say, "Thank you."
I smile a smile you cannot see,
making a new memory of you, for me.

You understand that I desire you,
spoil you. One day you will tell me
it is the right day to make love & we might
not. When you find the courage to want to,
I will reach out to you. You will laugh at me
for something I tell you. I do not question
the kind of lovers we might be.

Morning text from you

Am feeling it.

For the editor, a poem

My poem is about writing
a poem & the pronoun
you are suspicious of is I.

It captures the exact moment
my feelings bend overtly
toward the other pronoun.

She is wet with feelings.
You say you almost never publish verse
about what we do before daylight.

I live but once

I live but once.
I have loved before,

& as love goes,
so goes love

like frost upon
winter fescue.

As love is,
so am I.

I am a icicle guest
in your soul.

I melt
within the warmth

of your body.

Unknown number

Maybe I was curious when I answered.
It was my ex-wife calling out of the blue
as the saying goes, & she asked me
several personal things before telling me
she wanted to have a baby next year.

As she talked, she said the baby she wanted
had to be mine.

I have not been like that she said
with any man but you.

She asked me about the blue car
with snow on it
& the woman in the picture
& wanted to know why I came
to Jamaica & did not visit her.

That would have been too painful
I said *after the things you did.*

I'm sorry she said.

Don't be sorry I said.
The past seems far away.

This is my number she said.
Call me if you decide you want to talk.

I do not tell her I will never call.

Pictures

I take a picture of you
while you lie on the bed
with your laptop.

An orb covers your body.
I walk around the bed
& take a second picture.

The orb hovers over your feet.
I go to the foot of the bed.
I take a third picture.

The orb rises between us,
shaped like a penis,
erect, crooked.

If you would change

If you would change anything
about life,

would you change lovers
like you change shoes

or your hair color
because you are depressed

or would you keep
your lover,

for he is as comfortable
as some old shoes

you cannot bring yourself
to discard?

January 2, 2014

I began to type the title
& it appeared magically

as tho the mind
within the computer

were mine.

We both know
there is no mind

within my computer.
It is programmed

to complete dates
& correct misspellings,

but I alone
know that I meant

to write about your text
to me early last week

when 2013 was receding.
I had a mind

to write:
am feeling it, too.

You get your wish

The snow,
with flakes
as large
as coins,
blown by a
January
northwest wind
is beautiful.

I imagine
that you
lie in bed,
motionless
beneath your
electric blanket.

The snow
ends
suddenly.
You will
not know
until you read
this poem
how fickle
a wish or
a dream can be.